MOVIES MOVIES MOVIES

MOVIES MOVIES MOVIES

An Entertainment of Great Film Cartoons

Edited by S. Gross

HarperPerennial

A Division of HarperCollins*Publishers*

MOVIES, MOVIES, MOVIES. Copyright © 1989 by S. Gross. All rights reserved. Printed in the United States of America. No part of this book may be used or reproduced in any manner whatsoever without written permission except in the case of brief quotations embodied in critical articles and reviews. For information address HarperCollins Publishers, 10 East 53rd Street, New York, NY 10022.

First HarperPerennial edition published 1990.

LIBRARY OF CONGRESS CATALOG CARD NUMBER 89-45041

ISBN 0-06-092012-2 (pbk.)

90 91 92 93 94 HOR 10 9 8 7 6 5 4 3 2 1

S. GROSS

"Cut...print...and get me down!"

PETER PORGES

MORT GERBERG

"He doesn't want to end up like Nanook. He wants points."

LAW OF THE UNIVERSE # 8,407

CINE-MATIC

E. SUBITZKY
ED SUBITSKY

If you put enough people in a theatre lobby, sooner or later one of them will say the word "Cinematic".

ED FISHER
© 1957 The New Yorker Magazine, Inc.

"—And then he promised to get me into documentary films."

"Hey! Gene Kelly! Debbie Reynolds here would like to go home, make herself some tea, go to bed and get some sleep."

MICK STEVENS

DON OREHEK

"Ask him to do his impression of George Raft."

"Say, wasn't there someone else sitting there yesterday?"

ALEX NOEL WATSON

JACK ZIEGLER

8

"Oh, darn it! Subtitles!"

"You asked me that yesterday. No, I didn't happen to see the Marx Brothers in 'The Cocoanuts.'"

10

"Would you consider a cameo role?"

JACK ZIEGLER

11

"How do you do. I'm Jiri Tromisik. I act in movies in Yugoslavia.
I'm dubbed."

"What this place needs is
a film festival."

"I'm a screenwriter. What do youse do?"

ED FRASCINO

13

BERNARD SCHOENBAUM

14

INDIVIDUAL FEATURES OF THE
BETTE DAVIS DEFENSE PLAN

"Dark Victory":
Our enemies will not only be struck down with inoperable brain tumors, but will fall in love with their doctors, which will make it worse.

Uhoh!

"Now, Voyager":
Thousands of domineering, manipulative mothers will take over households in unfriendly territories, causing everyone to lose their feelings of self-worth.

♪ Everybody hates me, Nobody likes me, Guess I'll go eat WORMS. ♫ ♪

"All About Eve":
Hostile areas will be invaded by seemingly defenseless, fawning, scheming beings who will stop at nothing to get their way.

Not that my opinion is worth anything, but I love your sweater! Then again, I love all your sweaters. You always have the best taste in sweaters. I mean that.

R. Chast

ROZ CHAST

15

"Come on out, Luke! I know you're in there!"

EVERETT OPIE

"I've come across this a lot in aging movie cartoon characters, Pookie.
The jerky motion and the facial paralysis; it's being caused by limited animation."

MARK HEATH

17

"Am I art?"

RICH RICE

CHARLES ALMON

"This is Vera. She'll dub your singing. Marge, she'll do your long shot dancing; Maxine, your stunts; and Jennifer's your body double."

"What kind of party is this supposed to be? 'The Corn Is Green' or 'Brief Encounter?'"

CINEMA VERITE

MICK STEVENS

21

3.

SERGIO ARAGONES

AIRPORT→
(NOT THE MOVIE)

MISCHA RICHTER

23

24

"I'm afraid the rest of your scene ended up on the cutting room floor again, sweetie."

PETER PORGES

HERBERT GOLDBERG

"Maud!"   "Harold!"

E. SUBITZKY
ED SUBITSKY

"Don't you just hate it when the screen breaks?"

"Quit complaining! You knew my life was film noir when you married me."

27

MORT GERBERG

28   "Make it more disastrous."

LOW BUDGET
'2001'

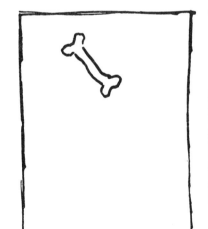
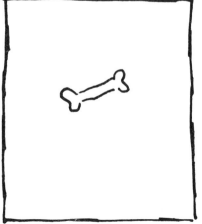

SIDNEY HARRIS

"There isn't any line for the movie.
This is for the video rental store around the corner."

30   ED FRASCINO

"Damn it, Busby. Must you take your work home with you?"

"Why? You cross the road because it's in the script! That's why."

"In Theatre One we're pleased to present 'Heaven's Gate.'   In Theatre Two we're pleased to present 'Ishtar.'"

EXCURSIONS

RICK GEARY
©84

A STUDIO TOUR

A REMNANT OF HOLLYWOOD'S GOLDEN AGE—NOW OPEN TO THE PUBLIC.

ALL ABOARD!

THE MOST GLAMOROUS NAMES IN THE BUSINESS WORK HERE DAILY.

HERE'S A HOUSE WE'VE SEEN IN COUNTLESS TV SHOWS.

THERE'S AN ACTUAL MOTION PICTURE IN PRODUCTION RIGHT NOW!

BURT LANCASTER ONCE STOOD HERE.

LUNCHEON IN THE COMMISSARY.

IF WE LINGER OVER OUR COFFEE, A FAMOUS FACE IS BOUND TO COME BY.

OH WELL.... MAYBE NEXT TIME.

ELDON DEDINI
© 1957 The New Yorker Magazine, Inc.

"Now, for instance, why aren't *those* kids at a Saturday matinee?"

"Pan left, stop, now pan slowly right, stop, zoom in on champagne, flowers, gifts, etc., pull back slowly and bring up music. She speaks."

BRIAN SAVAGE

37

"Do you realize you always tease the cat after a Kurosawa movie?"

CHARLES SAUERS

"All those in favor of saying 'It's a wrap' instead of 'Meeting adjourned' say 'Aye.'"

LEO CULLUM

38

"For God's sake, Lance. You always start singing 'Hurray for Hollywood'
and then you can't remember the rest of it."

"If our technology is so much more advanced than theirs,
how come *we* don't have in-flight movies?"

"Isn't that a terribly dangerous sport for a man your age?
Going to Cannes for the annual running of the starlets?"

MORT GERBERG

41

"Pardon me, gentlemen, but how would you like to be in a film about life in America today?"

BARNEY TOBEY
© 1970 The New Yorker Magazine, Inc.

"Unless I miss my guess, we should be nearing Errol Flynn's prints now."

MARTY MURPHY

BRIAN SAVAGE

ATTENTION!!
Parler pendant
un film de
Jerry Lewis
est un crime
serieux puni-
sable par la
peine de mort.

SIPRESS
DAVID SIPRESS

"The ex-starlets who intend to plead guilty to shoplifting
in Beverly Hills boutiques last weekend,
please step forward."

1.

2.

3.

4.

5.

6.

VAHAN SHIRVANIAN

"I hate previews. That's when the producers become religious."

BILL WOODMAN

47

"Leftovers from the Kiddie Matinee."

"Now get out there and sell movies."

SIDNEY HARRIS

"Well, at least it was true to life."

CHARLES ADDAMS

S. GROSS

JERRY MARCUS

"You know, the movie next door sounds a lot more interesting!"

E SUBITZKY
ED SUBITSKY

"Sir, the beginning of your movie is
being shown tonight in Cinema 7, the
middle in Cinema 9, and the ending,
I believe, in Cinema 21...."

54

GAHAN WILSON

"Small, medium, large or 'Gone With the Wind' supply?"

55

SIDNEY HARRIS

"In this film I portray an ordinary person dealing with everyday problems."

57

MOVIE CRITICS ON OTHER PLANETS

"It's me! Tarzan! I'm back from Hollywood!"

"Of course I'm over budget!
I have to sit and wait for a
goddamn fiddler crab to mate!"

PETER PORGES

59

BERNARD SCHOENBAUM

"Now go out and win one for the guppy!"

DON TUDGE'S
POSITIVE
MOVIE REVIEWS

KEY:
★★★★ =
Sheer perfection
★★★ =
Really, really great
★★ =
Terrific
★ -
Pretty damn swell

ATTACK OF THE CRANKY MUMMIES

If you like special effects as much as I do, you'll love "Cranky Mummies."
★★★★

LITE 'N' LAFFY

A wacky, rollicking romp that takes place entirely within a lamp store. Laughed till my sides ached.
★★★

HE SAYS, SHE SAYS, ETC.

Cinematic portrayal of a marriage on the rocks. Wept from the first scene to the last.

HORMONE HIGH

Is there anyone out there who doesn't like films about teen-age stereotypes?

★ ★ ★ ★

"Footage, footage, footage...."

"Tickets to the New Vision Feminist Film Festival! Oh, Ned, you shouldn't have!"

JOHN JONIK

65

S. GROSS

DONALD REILLY

"Why should I give you ten bucks for sound film? What's your track record?"

"Hollywood has never *dared* to deal with such an explosive subject!
Except once in 1947, in '56, and again in '72."

"Now, isn't this more fun than circling some old flame?"

BRIAN SAVAGE

"Give her the full starlet treatment—
clipped, capped, cupped, couched, and cast."

70

SIDNEY HARRIS

"I'd like to thank the director and the producer,
I'd like to thank my leading lady and my
supporting cast, but most of all I'd like to thank
Brad Glimmer, my make-up man."

SPECIAL EFFECTS DEPT.

Noel Watson

ALEX NOEL WATSON

ARAGONÉS

BRIAN SAVAGE

"So I tell this sweet young television actor, 'If you want roles in major movies, me bucko, you'll have to *come across*!' "

COSTUMES: DON ELSTON
SOUND: F. SKAFF
AUDIENCE: ED AINSMITH
MAY AINSMITH
BOB BARR
CLAIRE BRACK
LEON CADORE
EVE CADORE
S.T. CRANE
ANN CRANE
OTIS DAVIS
BILL DOAK
ANN DOYLE

SIDNEY HARRIS

"W. C. Fields is our mutual passion."

"This could only happen in Hollywood....
One night I'm selling popcorn at the Bijou; the next night I'm in bed with the projectionist."

OFF-BRAND WESTERNS

Welcome Wagon (1941) ~ Saga of a group of fun-loving folks who travel around to home of newly moved-in pioneers.

Trouble at Lo-Cal Ranch (1948) ~ Melodramatic tale of the first health spa-type spread of the Old West.

This tastes like boiled nothing!

The Jerry James Story (1952) ~ Jesse's unmemorable brother is the subject of this 3½ hour epic.

R. Chast
ROZ CHAST

"You have the right to remain silent."

"We can't produce this. It'll make money."

"…Okay, that's it, folks. We'll dub in the crying at the studio."

HOWARD MARGULIES

"Cut! We've replaced this scene with a clever narrative."

LOU MYERS

"A little action!"

PASADENA

BURBANK

ANAHEIM

LOS ANGELES

GO HOLLYWOOD

S. GROSS

S. GROSS

MARK HEATH

"On the phone you said you were Ronnie Rat, not the voice of Ronnie Rat."

"Live and learn, Clarabelle."

"You'd think the least they could do is show us a movie!"

KEN WILKIE

THE END

(OF $30,000,000)

EXIT

E. SUBITZKY

ED SUBITSKY

"They say he's terribly rich. He makes blood for all the major studios."

CHARLES SAUERS

BRIAN SAVAGE

"Check today's mail for scripts, will you, dollbaby?"

"It has very low mileage. It was driven only in two Burt Reynolds movies."

"Gee, I'm sorry, honey. I was so busy thanking all the little people that I completely forgot about you."

91

"Do you have any 35 millimeter film?"

DICK OLDDEN

BOB WEBER

© 1988 The New Yorker Magazine, Inc.

"Must be some kind of cult movie."

GAHAN·WILSON

"It seems all we make lately are spin-offs from movies!"

"It's Baby Cassandra,
   here to renegotiate her contract."

BERNARD SCHOENBAUM

95

FELIPE GALINDO (FEGGO)

JOE MIRACHI

"Seven dollars for a movie? For that price it better
have lots of sex and violence."

"We could have afforded to eat there, but *no*, you had to buy a Hershey and some Goobers at the movies."

CHARLES ALMON

1.

2.

3.

SIDNEY HARRIS

DIR

DIRECTOR

ARAGONÉS

SERGIO ARAGONES

HENRY MARTIN

"Edna, this is Al Bosworth. Al knows what happened to all
the old movie stars and where they are today."

STUART LEEDS

"I don't see movies. I read film."

"But this is billed as a once in a lifetime movie experience."

THOMAS CHENEY

J. B. HANDELSMAN
© 1987 The New Yorker Magazine, Inc.

"You get out of line, Mitchell, and you'll never work in this town again.
By 'this town' I mean, of course, Hollywood."

"You colorized 'Casablanca.' How unfortunate."

105

CATHERINE SIRACUSA

Dumbo's Distant Cousins

BIMBO

RUMBO

MAMBO

DIMBO

RAMBO

ROZ CHAST

"The producer wants the dialogue changed from 'Hi, Mom' to 'Top of the world, Ma.'"

JACK ZIEGLER

HENRY MARTIN

109

"No, thanks. Somehow Satyajit Ray and Milk Duds don't seem right to me."

FRANK MODELL
© 1985 The New Yorker Magazine, Inc.

"I liked it better in '56 on the Big Screen."

MIKE TWOHY

"Why does she want to go back to Kansas where everything is in black-and-white?"

ED FRASCINO

"Actor Arlon Marmot—who's box office, and actress Darla Dobson—who's not."

113

1.

2.

3.

4.

114

VAHAN SHIRVANIAN

"Last night I had a low-budget dream. It took place entirely in the Bates Motel."

115

MICHAEL MASLIN
© 1985 The New Yorker Magazine, Inc.

"It wasn't the airplanes that killed him.
It was Woody Allen's anxiety-directed Bergmanesque remake."

ELDON DEDINI

117

118　　　"…And now the moment you've been waiting for all year—the nominees for Best Picture are…."

"My job is to take a tough Mexican-American kid, a Jewish kid from Brooklyn, a snooty Ivy Leaguer, a big ignorant farm boy, and a miserable drunk, and mold you into a second-rate World War I movie!"

BRIAN SAVAGE

119

"In the book she dies."